Black Hawk Down: The History of the Battle of Mogadısnu

By Charles River Editors

CW3 Michael Durant's helicopter (*Super Six-Four*) above Mogadishu on October 3, 1993

About Charles River Editors

Charles River Editors provides superior editing and original writing services across the digital publishing industry, with the expertise to create digital content for publishers across a vast range of subject matter. In addition to providing original digital content for third party publishers, we also republish civilization's greatest literary works, bringing them to new generations of readers via ebooks.

Sign up here to receive updates about free books as we publish them, and visit Our Kindle Author Page to browse today's free promotions and our most recently published Kindle titles.

Introduction

An American helicopter over Mogadishu in 1992

The Battle of Mogadishu (October 1993)

"The Somalis were a curious bunch. For every armed person, there were fifty unarmed just standing around, often right next to the guy firing at us." – Michael Goffena, a Black Hawk pilot

If it was the dawn of a new world order in the 1990s, it was one of American unilateralism. Throughout the decade, America's unrivaled power and the globalization of the world through technology like the Internet offered Americans a sense of security and a belief that the United States could accomplish anything. After the collapse of the Soviet Union, the United States was the world's only remaining superpower, and communism around the world began to decline. Moreover, since communism in the Soviet Union was not defeated by outside military force but collapsed from within, its draw as an alternative system to western capitalism and democracy was seriously weakened.

10 years after American Marines were killed in the notorious barracks explosion in Beirut during Lebanon's Civil War, American special operations forces were sent to Somalia at the behest of President Bill Clinton as part of "Operation Gothic Serpent". The goal set for the

American forces was to capture Somali warlord Mohamed Farrah Aidid and thus prevent him from continuing to perpetrate violence. There is an ancient and oft quoted Somali saying that in many ways sums up the outside perception of Somalia, a race that appears unchangeably wedded to warfare and internal conflict: "Me and my clan against my nation. Me and my family against the clan. Me and my brother against the family. Me against my brother."

Somalia crept into the general global consciousness during the early 1990s as yet another distant and incomprehensible bout of African warfare began to generate news images of biblical famine, but even that conflict may have been lumped in with the others if not for an unexpected turn of events in October 1993. On October 3, 1993, a small force conducted an operation in Mogadishu to arrest two of Aidid's leaders, but they were pinned down as they sought their way out. In the attack, 18 Americans were killed, and the Americans lost two Black Hawk choppers, and as if that wasn't enough, footage circulated of a few soldiers' bodies being mutilated and dragged through the dust for a crime no greater than attempting to feed the hungry masses and protect a nation from itself.

The attack later formed the basis for the movie *Black Hawk Down*, but in its immediate aftermath, President Clinton ordered the withdrawal of American forces days later. Somalia seemed to have taught Clinton a lesson in unilateralism, because he refused to stop the genocide in Rwanda the following year. It seemed he had learned that the U.S. could not intervene anywhere at any time.

Black Hawk Down: The History of the Battle of Mogadishu chronicles the story of one of the most notorious events of the 1990s. Along with pictures of important people, places, and events, you will learn about Black Hawk Down like never before, in no time at all.

Black Hawk Down: The History of the Battle of Mogadishu

About Charles River Editors

Introduction

Chapter 1: Somalia in the 1990s

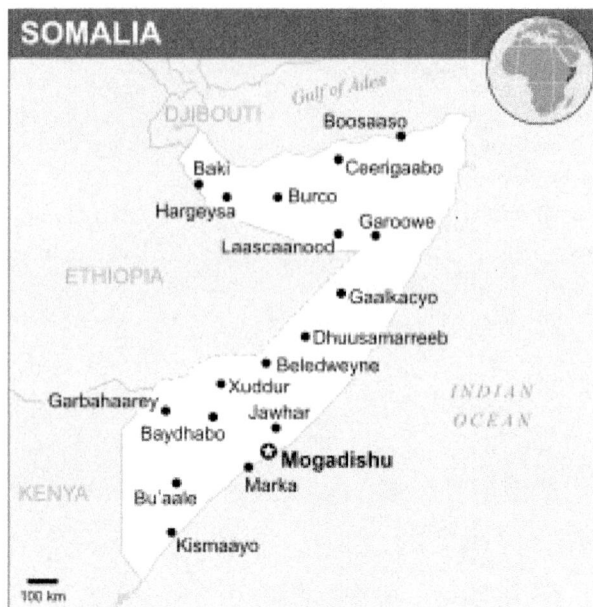

A map of Somalia

"In character, the Isa [a Somali clan] are childish and docile, cunning, and deficient in judgment, kind and fickle, good-humoured and irascible, warm-hearted, and infamous for cruelty and treachery." – Sir Richard Burton, *First Footsteps in Africa*

The territory of Greater Somalia fell under the colonial administrative mandate of Britain, Italy and Ethiopia.[1] Prior to World War II, Italian dictator Benito Mussolini seized the entire horn of Africa, fortifying the territory as a basis from which to link up with Italian Libya, positioning Italy to threaten British Egypt and the Sudan. The Italians, however, were roundly defeated by the Allies in North Africa, and in 1941 driven out of Africa altogether. Control of Greater Somalia then fell entirely into British hands. Many Italian colonists remained in the territory, however, and a United Nations trusteeship over the colony was eventually granted to Italy and Britain, with Britain tending to remain the senior partner until independence and unification in 1960.

Indigenous government in Somalia, however, was almost within itself an oxymoron.

---

[1] Note: Ethiopia at this time was recognized as a functioning dynastic monarchy in the European pattern, and was not initially subject to the threat of absolute colonial occupation

Traditionally no central government or unified control had ever taken root in Somalia. The nomadic lifestyle and individualistic mindset characteristic of ethnic Somali clansmen tended to precluded it, while historic attrition over water, livestock and other resources further complicated a bewildering ebb and flow of loyalties, enmities, alliances and conflicts. All of this spilled into post-independence politics with the inevitable result that the ideal of national unity was quickly subverted to narrow clan interests. A bloodless coup in October 1969, transferred power from civilian to military leadership, headed by army commander, Major General Mohamed Siad Barre.[2]

It is at this point that the fortunes of Somalia, now the Somali Democratic Republic, began to tilt. At first the signs were good. Siad Barre emphasized clan unity and development within a socialist framework that initially won him broad public support. Over the course of the next few years, however, clan disaffection and clan-based insurgencies became more widespread, until in 1992 a broad based alliance of opposition forces was formed under the banner of the Somali National Alliance (SNA). Several key figures emerged from this process, perhaps most notable of whom was General Mohamed Farrah Aidid, who would play a central role in the dramatic events of the next few years.

---

[2] Note: The coups were not entirely bloodless. It was precipitated by the assassination of President Abdirashid Ali Sharmarke by one of his own bodyguards.

Barre

Aidid

By the advent of the 1990s, popular discontent had spread throughout the country to the extent that President Siad Barre found himself facing a general revolt. At the head of the movement was General Aidid, who advanced towards the Somali capital Mogadishu from the Ethiopian border, capturing quantities of arms and equipment as he advanced. He entered Mogadishu late in December 1990. After that, Siad Barre fled the capital, taking with him everything that he could, and for a year or more he and Aidid grappled across the arid expanses of south/central Somalia.

A month after his ouster, Siad Barre attempted unsuccessfully to rally his forces and retake Mogadishu. Thereafter several bitter offensives played out as the embattled ex-president fought to regain the advantage. As he did he pursued a scorched earth policy across the region, destroying boreholes and canals, which disrupted the normal routines of agriculture, precipitating in large measure the desperate famine that would follow.[3] In May 1992, Siad Barre's depleted forces mounted a final offensive before the 73-year old ex-president fled to Kenya, where he settled briefly before being forced to seek refuge in Nigeria.

---

[3] Note: Heavy fighting took place around Kismayo and Baidoa, creating acute food insecurity in what later came to be known as the *Triangle of Death* in southern Somalia, demarcated generally by the settlements of Kismayo, Baidoa and Mogadishu.

In the meanwhile, the ouster of the old regime did not ultimately offer any relief for the Somali people, nor did it precipitate the emergence of democratic government. In fact, it had quite the opposite effect. Clan unity fractured at the moment that Siad Barre's army ceased to be a threat, at which point the strongmen and warlords turned on one another and a fresh war began.

Mohammed Farah Aidid had made the not unreasonable assumption that he, as the principal military leader and tactician of the revolution, would be poised to lead the country. However, effective control of the country remained with individual insurgent leaders in the various regions, and many of them resisted any efforts towards the establishment of a central authority. Moreover, fighting among the clans for local and regional control did much to exacerbate the conditions of famine that were by then being acutely felt throughout the south of the country and, to a lesser but growing extent, elsewhere.

The final, awful act of a bloody tragedy played out in the battle for Mogadishu. The two principal clan leaders, Aidid and Ali Mahdi Muhammad, turned against each other, each recognizing that control of Mogadishu was the key to control of the country. As 1991 drew to an end, both sides occupied quarters of the capital and girded for a final confrontation.

Ali Mahdi Muhammad

Fighting broke out in September 1991 and continued until February 1992, resulting in tens of thousands of deaths and effectively destroying the city that suffered under constant and random artillery bombardment for several months. With an absolute, and at times utterly incomprehensible indifference to human life, the struggle continued. The by now familiar images of the ruined boulevards of a once elegant city began to settle into the global consciousness as this human atrocity played out on television screens worldwide. Seeping into the reportage was equally stark imagery of human suffering on the fringes of city and in the deep hinterland, as the inevitable result of failed harvest and mass starvation began to seriously grip the countryside. The United Nations had long fled the capital, leaving just a handful of smaller agencies and relief organizations battling against astronomical odds to feed an exploding population of starving people.

An abandoned area of the city between the two sides in January 1993

Effective relief was impossible under these circumstances. Insecurity in southern Somalia was absolute. In the United Nations a strange lethargy prevailed as the outgoing Secretary General, Javier Pérez de Cuéllar, prepared to hand over to recently appointed Boutros Boutros-Ghali, possibly the worst possible choice of UN Secretary General that could have been made under the circumstance.[4] The situation in Somalia by the end of 1992 was almost incomprehensibly dire and seemed to demand attention, forcing a global leadership reluctant to involve itself militarily in Africa to do something, and fast.

Chapter 2: Military Background

Confronted by the situation in Somalia, the newly appointed Secretary General of the United Nations, Boutros Boutros-Ghali, found himself on the front line of the first major international crisis since the fall of the Berlin Wall. The collapse of communism in Europe altered the world in many ways, some obvious and some less so. In Africa, Cold War patronage fell away,

---

[4] Note: Mohammed Farah Aidid suffered from a deep personal enmity towards Boutros-Ghali for a variety of reasons, not least his belief that as Egyptian Minister of State for Foreign Affairs, Boutros-Ghali had been instrumental in Egypt's support of Siad Barre. This feeling appeared to have been reciprocated.

resulting in the collapse of many of the corrupt regimes that had survived solely as a consequence of Cold War superpower patronage. The United States was now the only remaining superpower, and its role in Africa, and in the developing world as a whole, shifted from the concerns of global power play to that of guardian of democracy and steward of economic recovery and good governance.

Boutros-Ghali

The Somalia crisis was the first major challenge to both the U.S. (in its revised role) and the UN as a body representative of a united global community. The UN, however, fumbled the Somalia issue, highlighting from the onset its inherent deficiencies as a highly bureaucratized, personality driven and procedure dependent organization. It also highlighted some of the unique and unexpected problems associated with peacekeeping, and peacemaking, in regions such as Africa where the normal tenets of humanitarianism appear to carry absolutely no currency. It was then, as it remains today, a source of astonishment to international bureaucrats and observers that it was the Somalis themselves who proved to be the defining obstacle against the provision of crisis relief to Somalia. Grassroots extortion and banditry dominated the catalogue of difficulties experienced by relief organizations, but qualitatively it was the politicization of food aid, and the difficulty of dealing with a constantly evolving latticework of clan alliances and enmities that underwrote most of the significant failures.

In most cases, food aid was simply stolen by anyone with an opportunity to do so, after which it was claimed and manipulated by individual clans and clan alliances to the detriment of others. Security in most cases was provided by the Somalis themselves, as a consequence of which humanitarian organizations had almost no control over where the food ended up once it had been landed. Militia gangs were contracted as technical staff but were essentially operating simple protection rackets, defining their own terms of employed through armed threat.

The net result was a calamity of haunting dimensions, and images of the crisis dominated foreign newsreels. International anguish was expressed through rolling debates and conferences in all of the major global forums, with a chorus of political lobbies, NGOs, religious groups and relief organizations adding urgency to a general call for emergency action in Somalia.

The first substantive UN move was to adopt Security Council Resolution 797, which endorsed Secretary General Boutros Boutros-Ghali's call for an emergency airlift of food to avert the very worst of the disaster. In support of this, President George H.W. Bush had authorized a US airlift – Operation Provide Relief – which utilized 10 USAF and US Air National Guard Lockheed C-130 Hercules transporters to air deliver some 48,000 tons of emergency food aid.[5]

---

[5] Note: Additional Canadian air assets were deployed under the separate but concurrent Operation *Deliverance*. A number of private chartered aircraft were used too.

A picture of Bush visiting Somalia

It quickly became apparent, however, that this crisis was far larger than a handful of emergency food drops, and indeed, statistics indicated a gradual worsening of the situation as the war continued. This led to the creation of UNOSOM, or the United Nations Operation in Somalia, the first active effort to militarily intervene in the crisis. UNOSOM was initially authorized at 500 men, in this case drawn from elements of the Pakistani Army operating under a limited mandate to secure the port, safeguard food shipments to and from the airport and escort food convoys.

Typically abstruse UN rules of engagement and its overtly political chain of command effectively hobbled the Pakistani contingent. In fact, without artillery, air support or heavy weapons, the Pakistanis were incapable of achieving anything at all. Operation Provide Relief, meanwhile, continued to airdrop food via a cost prohibitive and narrowly focused program aimed at providing the most basic emergency relief.

It was soon obvious that a more robust response would be necessary, and towards this end an international United Task Force (UNITAF) was authorized to bolster and support UNOSOM. Bearing in mind, however, that the bulwark of UNITAF was the U.S. Marine Corps, the mission was fundamentally an American effort. This effort was supported diplomatically by the appointment of ex-U.S. Ambassador to Somalia, Robert Oakley, as U.S. Special Envoy. Oakley was responsible for preparing the diplomatic ground for the arrival of UNITAF.

Oakley

UNITAF went ahead in three phases. The first was to secure Mogadishu, and the second and third aimed to secure the other major ports and the surrounding countryside. This was very quickly achieved, after which the distribution of food aid began in earnest. UNITAF was in almost every respect an American operation, with all coalition forces coming under US command. Diplomatically, however, it remained subservient to the UN as a strictly transitional operation, pending a resumption of responsibility by the UN in a second operation codenamed UNOSOM II.

UN Secretary General Boutros-Ghali, however, recognized fairly early on that UNOSOM II would be powerless to contain a resurgence of violence in Somalia without direct U.S. military support. He therefore attempted to impose a basic condition of general disarmament of the Somali faction before any large scale US withdrawal from the theatre would be considered. This immediately exposed a gulf between what the United Nations regarded as essential and what the United States recognized as possible.

The issue of disarmament was so fraught with difficulty that the question had been deliberately excluded from the terms of the mission, leaving the commander on the ground to determine according to local conditions what level of weapons control he felt was practical. In general the cantonment of heavy weapons and the removal of improvised fighting vehicles (colloquially known as "technicals") from the streets was considered acceptable. The seizure of weapons caches was undertaken if possible, individual weapons confiscated where necessary, and for the remainder an understanding was reached between UNITAF and the warlords that overt gunplay, or aggression of any sort, would result in a prompt slap-down, which, in rare instances, was precisely what happened.

A UNOSOM member's picture of an armed Somali "technical" in Mogadishu

In regard to the wholesale removal of weapons from the theater, it was simply not practical; too many weapons were in circulation and too much importance was placed on the individual right to bear arms. A second and perhaps more important factor was the level of insecurity countrywide, which ensured that disarming one clan simply ensured its destruction at the hands of a different clan. Another key point was that the veneer of cordiality between the U.S./UN and the warlords, under which the entire operation was proceeding, would be comprehensively shattered at the moment that a complete program of disarmament was rolled out. As a result, American military planners shied away from the whole idea, and quite reasonably so.

However, the protracted squabble that ensued over this issue succeeded only in delaying strategic planning. It seems that Boutros-Ghali genuinely believed that if enough pressure was maintained on the U.S. for long enough, the White House would acquiesce. This continued until April 1993, meaning, in practical terms, that the procedure-driven structure of the United Nations found itself dealing with a transition to UNOSOM II with no detailed plan in place.

It was here that the first glimmer of opportunity presented itself to the warlords. The official date of the handover was May 4, 1993, but by the time UN officials in Mogadishu received notification of this, the Marines had largely already departed. A sense of gloom descended over the local UN administration as the news sank in, and almost tangibly the dynamic military/civil partnership of UNITAF devolved into a bureaucratic and procedural regime replete with barriers and repetitions, as well as a general distancing from one another of the three principal branches of UNOSOM II (political, humanitarian and military). An overall sense that UNOSOM was ill-equipped to take on the task could not be shaken, coupled with the obvious fact that the Somalis recognized this too.[6]

If nothing else, the abrupt removal from the streets of Mogadishu of the hard-hitting U.S. Marine Corps had a profound effect on the Somalis that could not be dispelled even by the continued presence in the capital of the U.S. 10th Mountain Division, styled the Quick Reaction Force (QRF). Tangible signs of a drawing in of the UNOSOM peacekeeping role in Mogadishu were not lost on the Somalis. Day and night patrols were sharply reduced, and certainly the sight of nervous Pakistani units on the streets of the capital could hardly compensate for the removal of aggressive and well supported Marines patrols. Under the noses of UNOSOM, Aidid began to reinsert his heavy weaponry into Mogadishu, while broadcasts from his private radio station took on a noticeably more aggressive tone.[7]

At this point both the United Nations and the United States began to recognize Aidid himself as the main obstacle towards the successful implantation of Resolution 814.[8] The raising of tensions between UNOSOM and Aidid did nothing to deflect the inevitability of a contest of arms, and when Aidid was informed by UNOSOM on June 4, 1993 that the SNA weapons inventory would be inspected the following day, the stage was set.

---

[6] Note: Special Representative for Somalia to United Nations Secretary-General Admiral Jonathan Howe commented rather morbidly: *'The early may change of command marked the transformation of the force from one dominated by a superpower with more than 20,000 troops of its own on the ground to one led by a weak organization of many small contingents, the largest being 4,000 Pakistanis still waiting for a portion of their equipment'*

[7] Note: Under UNITAF a program of nation building had been under way for some time as an effort to empower village councils and traditional leaders as an alternative to the Kalashnikov diplomacy of Aidid and other warlords. This tended to marginalize the warlords, Aidid in particular, who was anxious to start pushing back the moment that the military muscle of UNITAF was withdrawn.

[8] Note: United Nations Security Council Resolution 814 authorised an extension of the United Nations Operation in Somalia II (UNOSOM II) until 31 October 1993

A Pakistani soldier in Somalia as part of UNOSOM II

The event had been preceded by widespread rumors that UNOSOM weapons inspections were a ruse, with the real objective being to target Radio Mogadishu, Aidid's radio station, which happened to be located at one of the five Authorized Weapons Storage Sites (AWWSS) that were earmarked for inspection.[9] Shutting down Aidid's main propaganda arm was certainly a general objective of UNOSOM, but it was not specifically part of the June 5 operation.

Trouble began at the radio station compound as a crowd of angry Somalis gathered during the inspection, presaging a tactic that would be increasingly in the weeks and months to come. An area would be flooded by women and children, and in the midst of it, a throng of militants would penetrate and attack while using the crowd as human shields. Despite this, the inspection proceeded successfully, but shortly afterwards a Pakistani escort unit ran into a carefully orchestrated ambush as it was heading back towards the main city stadium where Pakistani units were based. An intense firefight ensued, with the trapped convoy receiving large volumes of

---

[9] Note: It must be remembered that Somali civilian spies had comprehensively penetrated the UN structure, meaning that Aidid would have been fully appraised on UNOSOM plans as they were tabled, and suspecting that the target was his radios station, a major source of his power, he reacted accordingly.

small arms, automatic and rocket propelled grenade fire. Calls for reinforcements went out but were anticipated by the Somalis, who then ambushed relief vehicles. In the subsequent chaos, Italian helicopters inadvertently fired on their own side, while all over the battle periphery makeshift obstacles and roadblocks were positioned to hinder relieving forces. Scattered firefights took place as the fighting continued into the afternoon.

In the meanwhile, a second action took place as angry Somalis mobbed a Pakistani platoon guarding a food distribution site, shielding militiamen as they opened fire. By then, the hapless Pakistanis had already allowed the crowd to advance close enough to obstruct their weapons. Pinned down Pakistani units were eventually relieved by the Quick Reaction Forces and Italian armored units, but not before 24 Pakistani soldier had been killed and scores wounded and others captured. Three Americans and an Italian were also wounded.

An emergency debate was held in the Security Council the following day, resulting in the unanimous adoption of Security Council Resolution 837.[10] In that resolution, the United Nations appeared to accept without a formal inquiry Aidid's culpability for the attacks and authorized all necessary measures to bring to account those responsible. Implied in the resolution, although not specifically stated, was a go-ahead for the military steps that were subsequently taken against Aidid and his senior associates. It was a de facto declaration of war, at which point military operations gradually succeeded humanitarian operations as the main thrust of UNOSOM II.

The United Nations was now effectively fighting a counterinsurgency campaign.

Chapter 3: Leading Up to the Battle of Mogadishu

The irony of how things had evolved in Somalia since the iconic Marine landing of December 1992 could hardly be better illustrated than by a highly instructive observation made by Air Force Combat Controller Dan Schilling in a brief memoir of the iconic battle that occurred in the streets of Mogadishu on October 3-4, 1993. Schilling had just arrived in Mogadishu as part of Task Force Ranger and was observing a firefight underway between two rival Somali factions: "After requesting an MH-60 (Sikorsky UH-60 Black Hawk) from the JOC, I gave the aircraft that showed up a brief description of the situation down the road and asked him to do a flyby. He made a pass from our location over the Somalis and so was flying away from us. We were looking down the road at the gunfire being exchanged between the locals and then we watched in amazement as both sides stopped shooting at each other and began engaging the helicopter."[i]

In a few short months, the high minded humanitarianism that had inspired the United States and others to lend considerable weight to the alleviation of grotesque human suffering, created largely by the Somalis themselves, had gradually devolved into a situation where those trying to help were forced to fight, and pay in blood, for the privilege of doing so. However, if this

---

[10] Note: The resolution was drawn up in haste by US UN Ambassador Madeleine K. Albright in consultation with Anthony Lake and Ambassador Howe. General Colin Powell was not consulted.

appeared to defy Western logic, it certainly appeared to be completely rational to the Somalis, for it had not only been militias involved in the killing of the Pakistanis but large number of civilians too, even though civilians stood to benefit most from having peace imposed by the various coalition forces.

In the aftermath of June 5, numerous incidents of violence took place that resulted in scores of UNOSOM casualties and hundreds among the Somalis. On June 17, Moroccan peacekeepers sustained heavy casualties during an attack on Aidid's enclave in southern Mogadishu.[11] The last straw, however, was the August 8 detonation of a remote controlled device under a passing U.S. Army vehicle that killed four American Military Policemen, followed by a landmine explosion two weeks later that injured another six.

Soon afterwards, the decision was taken to form Task Force Ranger, a battle group comprising U.S. Army Delta Force, Ranger teams, an air element provided by the 160th Special Operations Aviation Regiment, four Navy SEAL operators from SEAL Team Six and members of the Air Force Pararescue/Air Force Combat Controllers, for the prosecution of what was codenamed Operation Gothic Serpent.[12] On August 22, 1993, Task Force Ranger made landfall in Mogadishu with a minimum of fanfare, and it promptly set about achieving the capture of Mohamed Farah Aidid and any known associates. The task force, commanded by Major General William Garrison, bypassed the established chain of command in Mogadishu and was answerable directly to CENTCOM. Major General Tom Montgomery, commander of U.S. forces in Somalia, had no direct authority at all and was simply kept informed as a matter of protocol.[13] Commander of Delta Force and Second in Command to Garrison was Colonel William Boykin.

---

[11] Note: The journalists were Hansi Krauss of Associated Press, and Dan Eldon, Hos Maina and Anthony Macharia, all of Reuters.

[12] Note: The key component of Task Force Ranger was the elements of 3 Ranger Battalion. There are three maneuver Ranger Battalions in the U.S. Army, all of which belong to the 75th Ranger Regiment, which is part of the United States *Special Operations Command*. Each of the Ranger Battalions is commanded by a lieutenant Colonel, falling directly under the command of the Ranger Regimental Commander. Ranger Battalions are based at three separate military installations. These are: 1st Ranger Battalion at Hunter Army Airfield, Savannah, Georgia; 2nd Ranger Battalion at Fort Lewis, Seattle-Tacoma, Washington; and 3rd Ranger Battalion at Fort Benning, Columbus, Georgia, the latter being the headquarters of the Ranger Regiment, which is commanded by a colonel. The three Ranger Battalions, alongside other integral but smaller elements, make the U.S. Army's sole Ranger Regiment (the 75th Ranger Regiment). Each battalion maintains high level of combat readiness at all times, with one of the three battalions designated as the *Ranger Ready Force 1* (RRF1) battalion. The (RRF1) battalion will be in RRF1 status for a period of two-month, twice annually. RRF1 status implies both the responsibility and the ability to deploy as a combat force anywhere in the world within eighteen hours after initial alert notification; a state of readiness commonly referred to as being on a 'short string'.

[13] Note: Major General William Garrison was at that time commander of **Joint Special Operations Command (JSOC)**, a component command of the **United States Special Operations Command** (USSOCOM), charged with the study of special operations requirements and techniques in order to ensure inter-operability and equipment standardization, to plan and conduct special operations exercises and training, and to develop *Joint Special Operations Tactics*. It was formed in 1980 in the aftermath of the failure of Operation Eagle Claw (operation to free American hostages in Iran).

Garrison

The decision to insert special operations forces into Somalia to take care of Aidid was arguably the main obstacle to the success of the UNOSOM operation. The decision was one not easily taken, and according to the Chairman of the Joint Chiefs of Staff, General Colin Powell, it was one that he was quickly come to regret. There were other decisions that Powell would regret, perhaps most importantly rejecting a request from commanders on the ground for the inclusion of Lockheed AC-130 gunships as part of the equipment earmarked for Operation Gothic Serpent.[14] The inclusion of this, and other heavy operation equipment such as tanks and armored personnel carriers (all of which were held back for fear of presenting too aggressive an image of American intentions in Somalia), might have altered the complexion of one of the toughest actions fought by American forces since the Tet Offensive of 1968, and it definitely would have saved lives.

The main force element of Task Force Ranger was drawn from the 3rd Ranger Battalion, commanded at that point by Colonel Danny McKnight. McKnight published a book some years later entitled *The Streets of Mogadishu: Leadership at its Best, Political Correctness at its Worst*, in which he fulminates quite openly on the damage done by an overly political decision-making process in the matter of defining the scope and direction of hazardous military operations such as Operation Gothic Serpent. Among the memoirs and analysis of this operation available today, McKnight is one of the few willing to acknowledge the nakedness of the king and admit that the

---

[14] Note: **Colin Powell:** *'In Late August, I reluctantly yielded to repeated requests from the field and recommended to [Les] Aspin that we dispatch the Ranger and Delta Force [an elite commando unit]. It was a decision I would later regret.'*

operation was a disaster. For that, he blames the political leadership, not unjustifiably.

McKnight

At the same time, pointing the finger of blame at the political decision-making process only tells part of the story because there were significant operational and tactical flaws evident as well, even at the time. Overconfidence might perhaps have been one of these; there was a tangible elitism among the Rangers and the other special force elements of the task force regarding their conventional army brethren of the 10th Mountain Division. The latter had already fought a number of actions in the streets of Mogadishu and had lost one Blackhawk helicopter to an RPG attack. Underestimating the fighting qualities and commitment of the enemy was another failure, and tactical predictability was perhaps the most dangerous.

Task Force Ranger touched down in Mogadishu on the evening of August 26, 1993, arriving aboard six giant C-5A Galaxy cargo jets. The arrival was greeted by Aidid's forces with a significant mortar barrage aimed at the main airport complex,[15] and Garrison decided to return the compliment hard and fast. Four days later, in the early hours of the morning, a dozen helicopters dropped a team of commandos on the roof of a building on the Via Lenin – Lig-Ligato House – rounding up and handcuffing the occupants in a matter of minutes.[16] The operation was seamlessly executed, but unfortunately it was later revealed that most of the captives were local UN staff members, underlining the importance and the difficulty of obtaining

---

[15] Note: Such mortar attacks were frequent, but usually inaccurate and seldom effective. The press had, however, been alerted to the arrival of Task Force Ranger, which meant, of course, that the fact was widely appreciated in Somalia too.

[16] Note: Prior to this TF elements had conducted a vehicular reconnaissance of Mogadishu, with air cover provided by the task force aviation element. This aggressive and highly confident display announced fairly unequivocally that new boys were in town. Aidid would obviously have been aware of what the job at hand was.

up-to-the-minute tactical intelligence in a highly fluid operational environment.[17]

The raid on the Lig-Ligato compound was the first of seven operations undertaken by Task Force Ranger in Mogadishu during its deployment, and the next operation very narrowly missed capturing Aidid. This operation again went smoothly; intelligence, despite being lean at the best, had on this occasion indicated accurately that the warlord was present, but perhaps sensing danger, he succeeded in slipping the net. At the same time, Aidid realized he was not playing with amateurs, and with a $25,000 bounty on his head, he knew his own people well enough to seek cover deep underground.[18]

Recognizing this, Major General Garrison opted to focus on Aidid's six top lieutenants – known as Tier One Personalities – upon the assumption that if the Americans couldn't take out the head, they should work on the body. At the top of this list was Osman Ali Atto, a wealthy Somali businessman and Aidid financial strategist. During the third week of September, Atto was spotted by chance in a vehicle and was lifted in a timely and smooth retrieval that was almost a textbook operation of its kind. Within minutes of information being passed back to the JOC, an AH-6 Little Bird helicopter appeared overhead and two sniper rounds were put into the engine block of the car. Moments later, commandos roped down from a hovering UH-60 Black Hawk and surrounded the target, taking Osman Atto into custody without incident.

[17] Note: In practical terms Somalia had reverted back to a pre-electronic age which tended to frustrate the high-tech intelligence gathering methods that the CIA had perfected in recent years, and the almost unbreakable clan bond, coupled with the awful ramifications of treachery, all tended to limit the flow of useful operational intelligence. Aidid himself was also highly mobile and extremely well camouflaged within the rat warrens of Mogadishu.

[18] Note: The reward was posted by Bir and Montgomery. The effect of it was to annoy Aidid and the Somalis that it was so paltry. Consider this against the (later) US$25 million posted on the head of Osama Bin Laden.

Atto

In the early hours of September 25, 1993, an incident occurred that was not considered significant at the time but would later be revisited as extremely important in regards to the events that followed. On a routine night reconnaissance mission, a QRF Blackhawk helicopter was hit by an RPG rocket as it passed close to Villa Somalia, the old Presidential Palace. The helicopter was flying at about 100 feet over the city, displaying no lights, and at a point when the moon had dropped below the level of the horizon. The rocket had struck the underbelly of the Blackhawk, igniting its fuel and quickly engulfing the cargo area in flame and forcing it down in the southern quarter of Mogadishu. The pilot struggled to maintain flight in order to reach the safety of the port area, and while three of the five crew members were killed instantly, the pilot and co-pilot survived and succeeded in reaching friendly lines.

Chapter 4: The Battle of Mogadishu

The crew of *Super 64* a month before the Battle of Mogadishu: (l-r) Winn Mahuron, Tommy Field, Bill Cleveland, Ray Frank and Mike Durant

The capture of Osman Ato was satisfying but perhaps counterproductive, as it rattled Aidid somewhat and forced him deeper underground. However, persistence seemed to pay off on October 3 when a call came in from a buried "asset" in Mogadishu indicating that a cadre of top Aidid lieutenants, including two from the Tier One list, was scheduled to meet that afternoon inside a compound located on Hawlwadig Road close to the Olympic Hotel. It was suggested that Aidid himself might attend.

Initial intelligence was received at about noon, after which indications began to circulate that an operation was afoot. For the moment, activity was focused in the operations center, as word was radioed back to the intelligence asset to position a driver on the street outside the target building. The asset was supposed to do this so that an Orion spy plane overhead, beaming real time video imagery onto screens in the operations centre, and surveillance Blackhawks, also constantly in the skies over Mogadishu, could pinpoint the exact location.

As Task Force Ranger busied itself for action, communications continued with the buried asset, who was displaying some reluctance to approach the actual target building and required some talking past his prevarication. At 15:00, a provisional go was given for the launch of the operation, although the signal for launch – codeword Irene – would not be given without 100% confirmation that the targets were in situ. Such confirmation was received at the Task Force Operations Center at approximately 15:30.

As a result, the Battle of Mogadishu occurred during the late afternoon, consuming the remainder of the day and the subsequent hours of darkness between October 3 and 4, 1993. Over the course of many hours, the fighting would evolve, with certain parallel sequences initiating a cascading cause and effect, all of which culminated in what was inescapably an operational fiasco.

The risks of the operation were not insignificant. Entering the heart of what was known as the Black Sea – the heart of SNA controlled turf – in broad daylight, after having exposed the Somalis militias to several general repetitions of the same tactics, was certainly very risky.[19] The timing also couldn't have been worse, as it was coming at a time of day when Somali militiamen, many of whom had been steadily migrating to the city in support of operations against the coalition, could be expected to be energetic and ready to fight.[20]

Planning for the operation on October 3 followed more or less the same pattern as previous operations. Four light MH-6J Little Bird helicopters would each carry four snipers, two externally seated on either side of the helicopter, and each of the Little Birds was armed with

---

[19] Note: A QRF Blackhawk had been shot down on 25 September by what was deemed to be a lucky RPG hit. There was, however, some suggestion made that perhaps the Somalis were adapting their response to the US commando strategy by flooding the field with RPGs and attempting to draw helicopters into an ambush. It was widely expected that if significant casualties could be wrought on US troops, a withdrawal would quickly follow.

[20] Note: Grown throughout the Horn of Africa and the Arabian Peninsula, *Khat*, known variously as Arabian tea, qat, gat, or miraa, is a green leaf plant, the chewing of which induces a mild sense of euphoria combined with the stimulant properties of hyper-alertness, talkativeness and general loss of appetite. Its traditional value has been as a social catalyst, not unlike alcohol, that offers a generally positive initial mood enhancement, followed, after several hours, by emotional depletion, instability, irritability and listlessness. Although not dissimilar in general pharmacological action to coffee, also popular in the region, the use of khat goes back much further, and certainly it remains in generally wider use as an indispensible social medium in a largely alcohol free environment. The question of the addictive qualities of khat remains an open debate, but it can be surmised by the extent to which the substance has become embedded in the day to day life of the region, and in expatriate communities worldwide, that some higher level of dependency is experienced by khat users that tends to prompt addictive responses.

rocket pods mounted beneath. Another four Little Birds, armed with 7.62 Miniguns and 2.75-inch rockets, would cover and protect the front and rear of the target building.[21] Delta C Squadron operatives would fast rope onto the roof of the target building from two Little Birds and penetrate the building and conduct a sweep and snatch. A hard-hitting force of eight UH-60 Blackhawk helicopters would follow, two of which would be carrying Delta assaulters and their ground command, and four of which would be loaded with a Ranger chalk – parlance for a specific aircraft load – to four points at each corner of the target building.[22] The Rangers would be inserted by fast rope and would immediately establish a security cordon. At the same time, a vehicle convoy would arrive alongside the target building, into which would be loaded the captives, the Delta Force operators, and the Ranger chalks for a quick and smooth extraction. All of this would be undertaken at lightning speed and ideally wrapped up before the Somali militias were able to effectively respond.

A picture of Little Birds

---

[21] Note: The **M134 Minigun** is a 7.62 mm, six-barreled machine gun with an extremely high rate of fire - some 2,000 to 6,000 rounds per minute – and which employs a Gatling-style system of rotating barrels powered by an electric motor.

[22] Note: The term *chalk* was first coined in World War II for airborne troops during Operation *Overlord*, the Allied invasion of Europe. The aircraft flight number was placed on the troops' backs with chalk. It was later used during the Vietnam War, when it was common practice to number with chalk the sides of the helicopters involved in an operation.

An American base in Somalia on October 3

An eighth Blackhawk would have on board two mission commanders, one coordinating the pilots and one directing the men on the ground. In addition, three OH-58D Kiowa helicopters, essentially a Bell helicopter configured for observation and direct fire support, would occupy the airspace above the target to provide real time audio and video of events on the ground directly to the Joint Operations Center (JOC). High above would be a P-3 Orion spy plane.

At 15:32, codeword Irene was issued and the mission began. The air flotilla lifted off for an estimated three minute flight to the target area,[23] and at more or less the same time, the ground convoy moved off.[24] At 15:40, two AH-6 Apache gunships ran a last minute flight over the target building before four MH-6 Little Bird attack helicopters dropped 16 Delta soldiers close to the building for the main assault. Moments later, two Blackhawks dropped off a further 30 special operations soldiers to conduct close-in security and assist the assault team.

As this was underway, four Ranger chalks, comprising about 16 men each, were fast roped into position in a highly choreographed sequence, but this was complicated by an almost immediate obscuring of the landing zone by a mass of dust and debris blown up from the unpaved streets below.[25] It was not immediately apparent to those troops exiting the hovering Blackhawks, but

---

[23] Note: Nineteen aircraft, twelve vehicles and 160 men

[24] Note: The ground convoy comprised seven Kevlar Humvees, two un-armored cargo Humvees and three five-ton trucks. The convoy was manned primarily by Ranger elements, but included Navy SEALs and a US Air Force Combat Controller.

robust enemy fire had begun immediately. Small arms hits were registered on the aircraft bodies and rotor blades, but it was when RPG airbursts began to be observed that the gravity of the situation abruptly became apparent. It was clear that the Somalis had been primed to respond to low level helicopter movement with a barrage of RPG fire, and it would only be a matter of time before a bird was hit.

The first three deployments went smoothly, but Chalk Four began to take heavy fire while still in the air and was roped in about block too far north of the intended drop point at the northeast corner road intersection. Under the circumstances, this was not critical, but it was complicated by a Ranger, PFC Blackburn, missing the rope and plunging 45 feet to the street below, sustaining serious neck, head and internal injuries. The injured Ranger was pulled out of the street and towards the waiting vehicles under a withering enfilade of enemy fire, and McKnight ordered that PFC Blackburn be evacuated back to base. The small group of vehicles selected for the mission survived a harrowing journey which cost the life of another soldier, Sergeant Dominick Pilla.

Overhead, pilots were already beginning to observe and report on a rapid and ongoing influx of militiamen and civilians into the area, with a resultant increase in hostile fire. It might not unreasonably be said that the Somali response to the operation had about it almost the character of a popular uprising.

---

[25] Note: The fast rope technique in use by US forces is an adapted of a British concept first used in a combat environment during the Falklands Campaign of 1982. It was used originally in a 'fire pole' style on a smooth nylon rope, but this has since been phased out in favor of a thick braided rope that is easier to grip. The only specialist equipment involved, besides the rope itself, is a pair of thick leather gloves to protect against rope burn. For the remainder the system relies on technique.

A picture of Rangers outside the target building on October 3

The ground convoy under the command of Lieutenant Colonel McKnight arrived in position without action or mishap, and soon after the departure of the medical evacuation convoy, the 24 captured Somalis were hurried out of the building in flex cuffs and bundled into the waiting vehicles.

However, as this was underway, and as the security perimeter devolved into a series of static firefights, the unthinkable happened. Number Super-61 Blackhawk, piloted by CW4 Cliff Wolcott, was hit under the main rotor by an RPG rocket and crashed at a location a few blocks north of the target building. Supporting aircraft immediately attempted to determine who if any of the crew and passengers had survived and to lay down suppressing fire to hold back the immediate onrush of Somali militiamen and civilians.

Naturally, it was at that point that the operation began to unravel, and word was immediately sent to the QRF located at the university compound to mobilize immediately. A wholly unexpected intensity of response was amplifying moment-by-moment as the militias organized and were reinforced by incoming members flooding in from all parts of the city and beyond. Makeshift barricades were being thrown up at key intersections while palls of black smoke from the customary burning tires were signaling far and wide that a significant engagement was underway.

The Rangers' creed - no man left behind - abruptly became the creed of the operation. Ranger units heavily engaged around the target building were now forced to contemplate moving north several blocks in order to secure the crash site, and the ground convoy, having sent back a detachment containing the injured PFC Blackburn to base, was further ordered to proceed to the crash site to retrieve survivors.

Thus began an almost unbelievably harrowing journey through a virtually ongoing ambush, and through streets obscured by dust, smoke and debris that were filled with astronomical volumes of incoming fire and obstructed wherever possible by roadblocks and other obstacles. Vainly attempting to follow instructions, Lieutenant Colonel Danny McKnight resolutely attempted the impossible until weighed down by casualties, and at the risk of becoming combat inoperable, he withdrew back to base through a gauntlet of hostile action.[26]

As McKnight's men were pushed back, an MH-6 Little Bird piloted by CWO's Karl Maier and Keith Jones dropped into the narrow confines of an urban crash scene, strung with wires and with a matter of inches of space to spare, and succeeded in rescuing two injured crew members while at the same time attracting a surge of hostile fire from converging Somali militiamen.[27]

---

[26] Note: Communications between the circling Orion Spy Plane, which was providing direction, and the floundering convoy were conveyed first through the JOC, which resulted in a 3 second delay in directional instructions being delivered to the ground, which in the fast moving action of the moment caused numerous wrong turns and obstructed routes, causing the convoy to lose itself in the city while consistently engaged in heavy combat.

Simultaneously, an advance party of Rangers comprising Chalk Two and part of Chalk One arrived on the scene, having fought their way up several city blocks at the cost of several wounded and one fatality (one of the wounded would later die at the crash site).

Moments later, around 16:48, a Combat Search & Rescue team arrived overhead and fast-roped in from a hovering Blackhawk, which itself took a direct hit from an RPG rocket. In one of the most celebrated actions of the operation, pilot Dan Jallota held the aircraft in a hover until the CSAR team was on the ground before limping off towards the airfield and crash landing.

All of this had taken place within less than an hour. The Delta and Ranger deployments had begun at 15:42, and Super-61 was brought down at 16:20, 40 minutes or so from the first arrival of American troops on the scene. By 16:30, Karl Maier and Keith Jones had lifted off with two casualties, Rangers had begun to form a security perimeter, and the Combat Search & Rescue Team had arrived and was attending to casualties, which were mounting steadily as the action progressed. By this point, the ground convoy was also on the move, fighting its way towards the scene while taking unrelenting enemy fire and finding no clear route to the site of the crash.

This combination of forces (CSAR Team, Ranger chalks and Delta soldiers) totaled approximately 90 men on the ground, and they held Crash Site One with ongoing helicopter assistance, all the while under constant and heavy fire. One of the dead pilots was removed from the wreckage, but the other could not be removed without equipment.

At 16:26, six minutes after the crash of the first helicopter, Super-64, piloted by CW4 Mike Durant, moved in to take the place of Super-62. Within 15 minutes of its arrival there, it too took a direct hit from an RPG rocket just below the tail rotor. It succeeded in staying briefly in the air but soon came down heavily, coming to rest approximately a mile southwest of the target building.

Once the second helicopter went down, the operation was plunged into crisis, and it was at this point that the denial of key assets – heavy operational armor and AC-130 gunships that would have provided vital suppressing fire – was most keenly felt. It is also worth noting that as Lieutenant Colonel McKnight toured the ambush alleys of Mogadishu in a confusion of delayed instructions, the AC-130s would have been able to provide real-time communications on the ground, which would almost certainly have saved lives and enabled the convoy to reach not only Crash Site One but very possibly Crash Site Two as well.

---

[27] Note: One WIA would later die of his injuries.

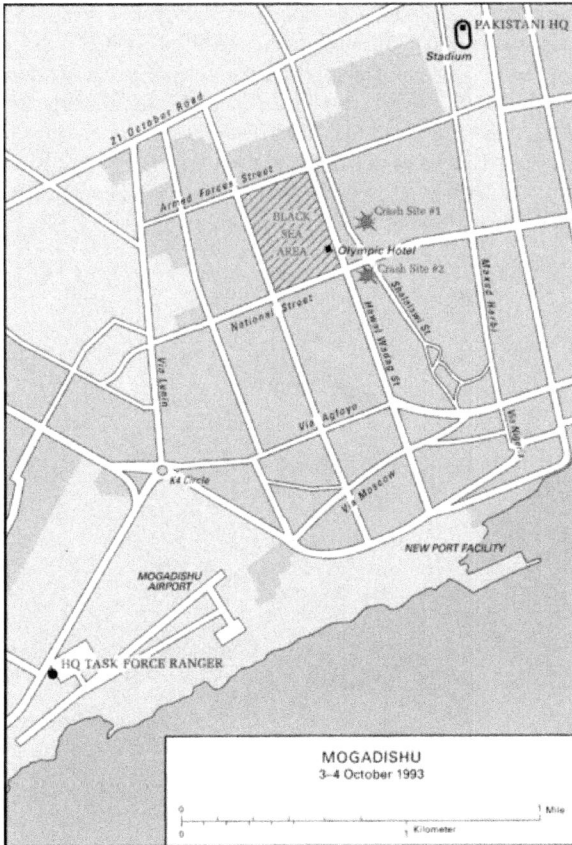

A map of the area of operations

Durant and his crew of three survived the crash, but they were all badly injured. Moreover, it was clear from the aircraft circling above that large numbers of armed and unarmed Somalis were converging on the scene and would overrun it within minutes. There was no immediate possibility of ground support, and air support was already overstretched dealing with three points of crisis - the battered and beleaguered ground convoy, still at that time battling through the streets of the city, and the two crash sites.

A moment of profound courage then followed. Providing sniper cover from the air were two Delta Force snipers, Sergeant First Class Randy Shughart and Master Sergeant Gary Gordon, but the two submitted repeated requests to JOC to be dropped into Crash Site Two to help defend it from the large numbers of Somalis drawing in. In due course, permission was given, and the two were inserted at a point some 100 yards or so from the crash site. Once on the scene, they extracted a badly wounded Durant from his pilot's seat, placing him in a position where he would be able to contribute to providing cover, and after attending as much as possible to the other crew members, those able to still fight did so to the death to defend the site. In the end, only Durant survived, and after dreadful mistreatment at the hands of the Somalis, he was retained as a captive/hostage by Aidid's forces. Shughart and Gordon were posthumously awarded the Congressional Medal of Honor for their actions that day.

Shughart

Gordon

As events unfolded, Aidid and his military captains learned about the ongoing fiasco quickly. The audacity of the Task Force Ranger assault had been premised on the smooth execution of the operation, which the SNA leadership had recognized very early could be easily derailed by the shooting down of an air asset, preferably a crew-served Blackhawk. Moreover, Aidid's men knew that the Americans would not engage unarmed civilians, allowing them the opportunity to use unarmed civilians as cover, and a downed aircraft would attract reinforcements, which in turn offered potential for even greater carnage.

Indeed, that is precisely what happened. The QRF, although it was not directly integrated into the order of battle, had been notified a full hour ahead of the launch of the assault that an operation was pending. Typically, no further indication would typically be given, but at 15:37, a REDCON ONE alert was received from Task Force Ranger headquarters, amplifying the state of readiness and hinting for the first time that Task Force Ranger might have tripped up. Then, at 16:30, minutes after the shooting down of Super-61, the call came for the QRF to present itself at the airport, where it would be placed under the command of Task Force Ranger Commander General William Garrison.[28] News was already making the rounds that Cliff Wolcott's Super-61 had gone down, and by 17:24, the men at the airport learned that Durant's Super-64 was also hit somewhere on the edges of the Black Sea. It was known that Ranger elements had already secured the first crash site, and that a significant battle was underway to hold it. Casualties had been taken and were continuing to be taken.

The status of Crash Site Two was still uncertain at this point. Gordon and Shughart were still alive and defending the position, but it was not anticipated that they could hold out for much longer. Thus, the QRF column, commanded by Lieutenant Colonel William David, was issued the unenviable and deceptively simple command to proceed from the airport grounds to secure Crash Site Two. The convoy ran into immediate and heavy enemy action as it left the airport, and it quickly met an ad hoc Ranger convoy racing in the other direction as it fled the tempest of fire and steel that it had sought to penetrate in response to the desperate situation.[29] That Ranger convoy had been ambushed almost from the moment it had left the security of the airport, and although coming within sight of the crash, it was unable to break through. The QRF convoy, consisting of Humvees and open five-ton trucks, was also unable to sustain any real forward momentum eventually had to fall back and return to the airport precinct at about 19:00.

As the situation unraveled, Major General Tom Montgomery, commander of U.S. forces in Somalia, began mustering UNOSOM's Malaysians and Pakistanis, now an extremely valuable asset with their tanks and armored troop carriers. Almost as soon as he stepped out of his bullet-ridden vehicle, Lieutenant Colonel David was told of a new plan involving two Malaysian APC companies and a Pakistani tank platoon.[30] This was the last resort, and an extremely difficult moment for the Task Force Ranger command. There had been no dearth of rivalry and derision traded between the armies of different countries, directed mainly at Task Force Ranger by others in the theater because of professional arrogance and isolationism, and the tendency of American forces in general to revel in the no-expense-spared nature of their equipment, training, support and command. The Americans tended to look down on the relatively modest capabilities of other armies, but now it was these exact troops who were mustering their archaic equipment to lend their weight to the extraction of Americans from a fiasco of their own making. At the same time,

---

[28] Note: The QRF was located at the University ground some three miles from the airport.

[29] Note: Reports differ on how long Gordon and Shughart were able to hold the site. According to one news report, the helicopter crew and two Delta snipers were able to hold the Somalis at bay for about two hours. Another report states that Shughart and Gordon were able to hold out for just 20 minutes. Bearing in mind the extraordinary efforts made by TF Ranger and the QRF to reach *Crash Site Two*, it seems unlikely that either would have been recalled before Crash Site Two was overrun, which tends to support the former theory.

[30] Note: These in the main consisted of West German made Condor APCs and US made M-48 tanks.

American command could have drawn no pleasure from the admission implicit in all of this that they were on their backs and being viciously mauled by a rag-tag militia armed in the main with AK-47s and RPG rockets.

Nonetheless, if the men besieged in the city were to be rescued, and some measure of credibility retrieved from the disaster, a convincing force had to me melded out these disparate units, even as the troops and commanders were understandably jittery about entering such a combat zone. It is a credit, however, to the control and forbearance of all involved that a viable force was eventually put together and ventured out of the port area and into the ongoing maelstrom of fire at about 23:30 that evening. The force consisted of the Malaysians and Pakistanis, two QRF companies, and a composite Ranger platoon made up of anyone and everyone willing to strap on armor, pick up a rifle, and climb on board.[31]

The 106-vehicle convoy began to take fire almost immediately, fighting its way slowly north up National Street towards an intersection where it was intended that the force would split up, with one detachment heading towards Crash Site Two and the other further north towards Crash Site One, where Ranger elements and surviving crew members were still engaged in an ongoing firefight. Some confusion resulted in two APCs becoming detached from the main group, with the lead vehicle being disabled by a direct RPG hit that also fatally wounded the driver. The QRF troops debussed and fought a tight defensive action for some time before it was able to link up with the main column again, costing the lives of two Americans and one Malaysian.

Eventually, the two crash sites were located, and it was apparent there were no visible survivors at Crash Site Two. The second withdrawal at Crash Site One was delayed considerably as the body of pilot Cliff Wolcott was cut from the wreckage of Super-61, but as dawn was rising over the smoke-filled capital, the column was finally able to begin its journey back towards safety. The final drama belonged to a small detachment of Rangers left to run beside the cover of the retreating armored vehicles, which, somewhat to their shame, made no attempt to maintain a compatible pace and quickly left the Rangers exposed to run the distance to the Pakistani Stadium unprotected. That has since been commemorated as the infamous Mogadishu Mile.

An extremely sad postscript to the Battle of Mogadishu occurred on Wednesday, October 6, two days after the battle. On that day, a single mortar round landed in the Task Force Ranger compound and injured 13 soldiers, one of whom, SFC Mathew L Reirson, a Delta operator from Iowa, died of his injuries.

Chapter 5: The Aftermath

The most memorable and regrettable aspect of the entire international intervention in Somalia

---

[31] Note: There was no enthusiasm on the part of either the Pakistanis or the Malaysians to send troops or assets into the Bakara Market area of Mogadishu, in particular in the midst of a deadly large scale mobilization of hostile militias. This was the area that had been effectively abandoned by UN forces upon the departure of the US Marines. Italian and Indian armor was also in theatre, but it was the Pakistanis and Malaysians that were more immediately available, and as a consequence they that came under enormous pressure to respond.

took place as the sun rose across the battle-scarred city of Mogadishu on October 4. This time, instead of images of starving children, footage captured Somalians dragging the bodies of slain American servicemen through the dusty streets of Mogadishu. The corpses were accompanied by a baying, jeering mob of otherwise ordinary civilians, kicking and abusing soldiers whose sole transgression, it seems, had been to attempt to save a nation from itself. In all, 18 Americans died in the fighting and 75 were injured, many seriously. Several hundred Somalis had also been killed.

It almost goes without saying that the political fallout in the aftermath of the battle was considerable. The Secretary General of the United Nations may have been tempted to point out his concerns to American officials, but any such sentiment would've been tempered quickly when the news came that a decision had been made to withdraw Americans troops altogether. On October 6, two days after the battle, Clinton convened an urgent policy review session, the result of which was a radically revised policy and a date selected for the withdrawal of all American forces from Somalia. Clinton personally ordered the acting chairman of the Joint Chiefs of Staff, Admiral David E Jeremiah, to desist from any further operations against Aidid in particular and any other Somali faction except in self defense. Aidid subsequently recognized this as being a rare moment when violence would not be the preferred policy and kept his guns silent, declaring a unilateral ceasefire as the inevitable process of disengagement was rolled out. The surge that followed was simply to protect those troops already in the theater and to more easily expedite the general withdrawal.

Among the warlords (and the militant Somalis in general), there was a great deal of crowing over the defeat of a might superpower, but in reality, the decision to withdraw was more prosaic and premised simply on the fact that Somalia offered almost zero strategic value to the United States. The episode was nonetheless a valuable lesson in the unforeseen difficulties of intervention, and it would have further ramifications after the explosion of ethnic violence that occurred in Rwanda the following year. Despite being well aware of the potential for genocide in Rwanda, Clinton's administration chose not to intervene.

All the while, Clinton defended the overall policy in Somalia while acknowledging that it had been a mistake for American forces to be drawn so deeply into a personalized and extremely costly quest to pluck Aidid out of the picture.[32] The re-appointment of Robert Oakley as special envoy underlined the administration's determination now to pursue a diplomatic solution, and as quixotic as it might seem, this was to be focused on political reconciliation involving all Somali factions. The decision to re-engage Oakley in tandem with a massive force buildup more or less signaled a return to the UNITAF policy of a big stick held in abeyance behind a substantial

---

[32] Note: To the extent that is was possible, Clinton washed his hands of the episode. In a May 1994 discussion with family members of the Rangers killed, he is reported to have express dismay that the operation was authorized and mounted after he had himself stated his preference for a diplomatic solution. This fact was revealed in an extremely thoughtful and insightful article published on May 13, 1994, by Michael R Gordon, Chief Military Correspondent with the *New York Times*, who revealed quite the extent to which US military officers had been divided over the raid that sparked the Battle of Mogadishu.

diplomatic carrot. Needless to say, within a military establishment already jaded against Clinton, this did not go down well.

The extent to which there had been a disconnect at the highest level over the decision to specifically target Aidid was revealed during a hearing of the Senate Armed Services Committee the following May, during which testimony was heard from a number of sources. Major General Thomas Montgomery, while defending the effort to capture Aidid, conceded that 'military superiors in the United States had been dubious about the mission'.[ii] According to Chief Military Correspondent to the New York Times, Michael R Gordon, "In defending the effort to capture General Aidid, General Montgomery said that the United States had good intelligence on the Somali warlord and that the military assessment was that the capture of the Somali strongman was necessary to break the back of the Somali resistance thwarting the United Nations. In doing so, General Montgomery acknowledged, he differed with Gen. Joseph P. Hoar, the head of the United States Central Command, and Gen. Colin L. Powell, then Chairman of the Joint Chiefs of Staff."[iii]

Also testifying was General William Garrison, whose principal point was the potential advantage that would have been gained during the crucial sequences of battle if his request for AC-30 gunships had not been rejected. Garrison admitted it was unlikely that he would have made use of armor during the original phases of the operation, but it certainly would have expedited the rescue had this equipment been available. The fact that helicopter gunships were required to hover at an average of 75 feet above ground in order to direct their fire made them extremely vulnerable targets, a risk that would not have been run by an AC-30 gunship, which would, in addition to the obvious physiological effect on the enemy, have simplified the response to the downed Blackhawks. It's possible if not probable that no helicopters would have been hit at all under the cover of one or more AC-30s.

In the end, blame was laid at the feet of the United Nations, and those within the Clinton administration who had allowed themselves to be influenced by the world body in the decisions that were made pertaining to military preparedness in the theater. Most frequently named were General Colin Powell himself, who appeared to obfuscate quite considerably, and Secretary of Defense Les Aspin, who also seemed more concerned with the appearance and political effect of too overt a buildup of force in Somalia despite authorizing the use of what force did exist on the ground in a proactive manner.

In a Senate Report released in October 1995, a great deal of space was taken up with various criticisms related to the decision not to send AC-30 gunships to Somalia. The Senate report was authored by two senior members of the Senate Armed Services Committee, Senators John Warner and Carl Levin, who wrote, 'The AC-130s were part of all the force package options and were included in all of the training exercises. This decision is inconsistent with the principle that you fight as you train."[33]

Les Aspin, in the midst of much general criticism, suffered censure for poor risk assessment in light of the number of similar operations conducted prior to October 3, and for not alerting General Garrison to both the policy shift towards a political solution and the enhanced risk of tactical predictability. "Had Aspin either reassessed the risk of each TFR operation more thoroughly or done a better job coordinating the policy shift in light of the increased risks, it is likely that the 3 October raid would not have occurred."[iv]

Aspin

From an outsider's view, this would seem to be grossly unfair given that Aspin was a civilian and Garrison was a seasoned military professional who should have been aware of the practical risks and should have instinctively understood the danger of repeating the same tactics more than once. In a situation where troops were so enormously outnumbered and thus relying on lightning speed and surprise, using similar tactics is even more unforgivable. Even with rudimentary communications, the Somalis would be aware within minutes of the launch that a raid was underway; and if it could be predicted what form the raid would take, RPGs would quite naturally be strategically deployed with a view to targeting the helicopters, which would almost

---

[33] Note: AC-130s had been deployed, and used, in recent UNOSOM actions, but the excess of collateral damage prompted a redeployment. This was seen by Aidid as a victory, and thanks to the 'CNN' factor, there was a reluctance to redeploy it back into the theatre.

inevitably be in low orbit over the target area.

Nonetheless, Aspin appeared to take the fall for Mogadishu and other failed aspects of the administration's foreign policy. He resigned for personal reasons later that year, but it should be clear that the fiasco of October 3 cannot be blamed on one man's fumbling of key security decisions. The failure was multi-faceted and can be traced from the highest decision making level, through the chain of command, and all the way down to a basic tactical level. On a strategic level, it was a failure of state policy, but on a command level, it was a failure of generals to prioritize military concerns over political ones. On a tactical level, there was a failure to anticipate and adapt.[34]

From a military point of view, it is the analysis of the latter that is the most interesting. The first point worth noting is that the local and central military command (the latter responding in part to political concerns) suffered a communication disconnect. The Clinton administration had assumed office without a coherent plan for Somalia, and while a purely military solution was initially sought, the policy had evolved into one of military containment and pressure while a political solution was sought. This fact was not communicated to the men on the ground, and it is conceivable that had Major General Garrison been aware that Aidid's value as a target had diminished, the Battle of Mogadishu would not have taken place at all. This, perhaps arguably, is where Les Aspin certainly can be held to fault.

It is also worth mentioning that the main force behind the deployment of Task Force Ranger for the purpose of capturing Aidid was an extension of a policy first established by Retired Admiral Jonathan Howe, a UN Special Representative who had initially driven that policy with the UN forces available to him. Once he knew this was impossible, he lobbied hard among friends and connections in Washington for the deployment of Delta Force, which Clinton ultimately did.

Ironically, almost exactly around the time the fateful October 3 operation begun, Howe arrived in the skies over Mogadishu upon returning from Djibouti and Addis Ababa, where he had been party to efforts to find a way of diplomatically dealing with Aidid. At this point, it was known that Aidid was willing to negotiate; he had contacted Jimmy Carter and expressed a desire for the former president and veteran diplomat to intervene on his behalf by means of an independent commission, going as far as to propose a negotiated solution to his standoff with the United Nations. Carter presented this approach to Clinton, who received it warmly. It seems strange, then, that this was the understood situation at precisely the time that Task Force Ranger was tearing up Mogadishu in an aggressive search for Aidid.

---

[34] Note: The Battle of Mogadishu has in fact never been acknowledged as a defeat, which in strict terms it was not. The objective was achieved and all troops were returned. This, however, does not detract from the fact that it did precede the collapse of UNOSOM, which handed Aidid a *de facto* victory that he could not claim on the battlefield. There are no accurate figures as to how many Somali fighters and civilians died during the battle, with estimates ranging between 300 and 1000 killed and many more wounded. Aidid was severely rattled by the events of October 3/4 and was closer to compromise as a consequence than at any time hitherto.

However, Garrison was working with what he had. Putting aside any possible result that could have been achieved had there been American armor and additional air support available, most battlefield analysis conclude that Garrison had what he needed available to him to successfully execute the operations. If anything, it was the allocation of those resources that caused the failure. Upon the launch of Operation Gothic Serpent, Garrison had accepted the removal from the initial Ranger strength of a platoon, again for the sake of political appearances, on the understanding that the Quick Reaction Force would be available for security backup and reinforcement when required.

However, very little coordination was undertaken between the two units in order to successfully integrate them, and the QRF was kept more or less out of the loop. The QRF was informed on a superficial level but by no means regarded or treated as a necessary adjunct to the Rangers' capabilities.[35] Had the QRF been on immediate standby at the airport and not several miles away at the university compound, it would have been available and ready to deploy immediately to secure Crash Site Two before the Somalis were in a position to react.[36] In conjunction with that, a better coordination of other forces in the theater (the Pakistanis and Malaysians in particular) would have resulted in a much speedier and efficient deployment of available armor in the event of a catastrophe of this nature. Furthermore, the deployment of a single Combat Search & Rescue team suggested that only one search and rescue scenario was all that could conceivably occur. Bearing in mind the fact that the air was filled with low-flying air traffic and that the Somalis had already proven capable of coordinating RPG fire days earlier, the planning for the operation appears to have anticipated and planned for a best case scenario.[37]

This highlights the failure of Task Force Ranger to plan an operation that adequately protected its tactical advantage: helicopters. The most vulnerable of these were the relatively slow Blackhawks, which remained in close orbit and within RPG range for 40 minutes after the initial deployment of the assault force on the target building.[v] Initially, there did not appear to have been any reason to use the UH-60s in a troop support role; a more sensible approach would have moved the heavier helicopters out of range of ground fire soon after the drop off and relied on the faster and lighter Little Birds, using mini-guns and snipers to provide ground support. Even after Super-61 had gone down, and despite there being only one Combat Search & Rescue team available, UH-60s remained in the area supporting ground forces despite the fact that Little Birds

[35] Note: At a command level it seems that General Hoar shouldered the greatest responsibility for failing to ensure unity of effort between Garrison and Montgomery. Under the Goldwater-Nichols Act of 1986 he alone had the authority to ensure a coordination of effort between TF Ranger and the QRF. There were, however, a number of command and control anomalies throughout the UNOSOM II period. The logistical components of US forces in Somalia were under the operational control of the United Nations in the person of Montgomery while the QRF was commanded and controlled by CENTCOM. TF Ranger occupied a third Command and Control chain. Much of this was to ensure that US forces remained under US command.

[36] Note: This force would have been even better equipped if Aspin had approved the deployment of 4 M1s and 14 M2s as requested by Montgomery. The fact that the QRF was not included in any TFR contingency would in practical terms have limited the usefulness of this asset.

[37] Note: A week earlier a 10th Mountain Division UH-60 had been shot down by a Somali RPG while flying at 130 knots, at rooftop level and at night; and during the sixth TFR raid on 21 September 1993, that captured Osman Atto, about fifteen RPGs had fired on TFR helicopters. Clearly this implied that the Somalis were targeting helicopters.

were available.

Of course, the Battle of Mogadishu is best known as Black Hawk Down for a reason, and the Americans' worst lapse was the lack of recognition at the JOC level that the Somalis were actively targeting helicopters and actually capable of shooting them down. Mark Bowden, who wrote the definitive history of the Battle of Mogadishu in his book *Black Hawk Down*, explained, "The QRF Blackhawk that had gone down the week before had been hit by an RPG. It had burst into flames on impact. That incident started everybody rethinking the way they had been doing things, even though the task force's six missions had gone without a hitch. Some of the pilots began agitating for more flexibility, but their commanders wanted them to stick to the template."[vi]

If this was so, then Garrison is certainly guilty of tactical inflexibility. He may have justifiably believed that the downing of the QRF Courage-53 had been a lucky shot; after all, that incident took place on a moonless night while the helicopter was flying without lights. However, that incident provided plenty of evidence that the SNA might deliberately be targeting helicopters, and that evidence went unheeded until it was too late to save 18 American soldiers.

Online Resources

Boko Haram: The History of Africa's Most Notorious Terrorist Group by Charles River Editors

Joseph Kony & The Lord's Resistance Army: The History of Africa's Most Notorious Guerrillas by Charles River Editors

Bibliography

Allard, Colonel Kenneth, Somalia Operations: Lessons Learned, National Defense University Press (1995).

Bowden, Mark (1999). Black Hawk Down: A Story of Modern War. Atlantic Monthly Press.

Boykin, William (Maj. Gen.), Never Surrender, Faith Words, New York, NY, (2008).

Chun, Clayton K.S., Gothic Serpent: Black Hawk Down, Mogadishu 1993. Osprey Raid Series #31. Osprey Publishing (2012). ISBN 9781849085847

Clarke, Walter, and Herbst, Jeffrey, editors, Learning from Somalia: The Lessons of Armed Humanitarian Intervention, Westview Press (1997).

Durant, Michael (CWO4), In the Company of Heroes, (2003 hb, 2006 pb).

Eversmann, Matthew (SSG) (2005). The Battle of Mogadishu: Firsthand Accounts from the Men of Task Force Ranger. Presidio Press. ISBN 0345466683.

Gardner, Judith and el Bushra, Judy, editors, Somalia – The Untold Story: The War Through the Eyes of Somali Women, Pluto Press (2004).

O'Connell, James Patrick (SGT.), Survivor Gun Battle Mogadishu, US Army Special Forces. (New York City) (1993).

Prestowitz, Clyde, Rogue Nation: American Unilateralism and the Failure of Good Intentions, Basic Books (2003).

Sangvic, Roger, Battle of Mogadishu: Anatomy of a Failure, School of Advanced Military Studies, U.S. Army Command and General Staff College (1998).

Stevenson, Jonathan, Losing Mogadishu: Testing U.S. Policy in Somalia, Naval Institute Press (1995).

Stewart, Richard W., The United States Army in Somalia, 1992–1994, United States Army Center of Military History (2003).

Somalia: Good Intentions, Deadly Results, VHS, produced by KR Video and The Philadelphia Inquirer (1998).

Notes

[i] Schilling, Dan. *The Battle of Mogadishu: Firsthand Accounts From the Men of Task Force Ranger.* (Presido Press. New York, 2006) p184

[ii] Gordon, Michael R. *New York Times*, May 13, 1994. *US Officers were divided on Somali Raid.*

[iii] Ibid.

[iv] Monograph: BATTLE OF MOGADISHU: ANATOMY OF A FAILURE by Major Roger N. Sangvic

[v] Ibid.

[vi] Bowden, Mark. *Blackhawk Down.* (Bantam Press, London, 2000) p118/9

Printed in Great Britain
by Amazon